The

by Olivia Pierce
illustrated by Dave Klug

Printed in China

ISBN 10: 0-15-358469-6
ISBN 13: 978-0-15-358469-5

Ordering Options
ISBN 10: 0-15-358357-6 (Grade K Above-Level Collection)
ISBN 13: 978-0-15-358357-5 (Grade K Above-Level Collection)
ISBN 10: 0-15-360698-3 (package of 5)
ISBN 13: 978-0-15-360698-4 (package of 5)

1 1 12 13 14 15 0940 15 14 13 12 11 10

Come in and look in the bin.
What do you see in there?
It is a nest.

I see a nest in there.
What is in the nest?
Can you see it?

Do you see the egg in
the nest?
A chick is in the egg.
Will the chick come out?
It will, but not yet.

Here is the hen.
The hen will sit on the egg.
This is good for the egg.

The hen will sit and sit.
She will not go out in
the sun.
She has to sit on the egg.

The chick will give the egg a tap.
Tap, tap, tap!
The chick will come out.

The little chick got out.
Here is the chick.
It will get big like the hen.
It will run and have fun.